SUPER SUMS

Addition, Subtraction, Multiplication, and Division

Rob Colson

Children's Press®
An Imprint of Scholastic Inc.

Acknowledgments and Photo Credits

Library of Congress Cataloging-in-Publication Data
A CIP catalog record for this book is available from the Library of Congress.

Copyright © The Watts Publishing Group, 2016
First published by Franklin Watts 2016
Published in the United States by Scholastic Inc. 2018

Printed in China

1 2 3 4 5 6 7 8 9 10 R 27 26 25 24 23 22 21 20 19 18

Photo credits:
t-top, b-bottom, l-left, r-right, c-center, front cover-fc, back cover-bc
All images courtesy of Dreamstime.com unless indicated:
Inside front Bubbersbb; fc, bc Pablo631; fctr Sailorr; fctc, 20-21b Gonin; fctl, 10l Jankom; fccl Cjansuebsri; fccr, 29b Tehcheesiong; fcbr Kaymotec; bctl, 9b Skalapendra; bccr, 23b, 31tr wabeno; 1c, 15c, 29tr Nokkaew; 1cl, 14-15, 29tl Grafistart; 4l Leisuretime70; 5c Andreadonetti; 5cr Paulmichaelhughes; 5b Fabiobalbi; 5bc zenwae; 6-7b Dvmsimages; 7t Broker; 8b Mexrix; 9t Ognianmedarov; 13b Kaymotec; 16c Forplayday; 16br Dedmazay; 17t Alfonsodetomas; 18-19b Valentyn75; 22cl Frenc; 22b Dolphfyn; bccr, 25b Ronstik; 26l 578foot; 27b Dolgachov; 28b Fixzma; 32t Stylephotographs

Teaching Guide

Visit this Scholastic Web site to download the Teaching Guide for this series:
www.factsfornow.scholastic.com
Enter the keywords **Super Sums**

MIX
Paper from responsible sources
FSC
www.fsc.org
FSC® C104740

Contents

True Sums

The four main calculations, or operations, in math are addition, subtraction, division, and multiplication. Strictly speaking, all sums are additions. The word *sum* is short for *summation*, which means "adding up."

The order in which you add up the numbers does not matter:

$$4 + 7 = 7 + 4$$

$$(3 + 5) + 2 = 3 + (5 + 2) = (3 + 2) + 5$$

This can be very useful in making sums easier to do.

Aiming for Tens

There are a few mental tricks that can help you add up. Pick the ones that make sense to you. Adding 10s is easy to do, so you can look for ways to change your sum into tens. If you're adding a series of numbers, look for any that add up to 10 and do these first:

$$3 + 4 + 7 + 6 = (3 + 7) + (4 + 6) =$$
$$10 + 10 = 20$$

Sometimes, rounding to the nearest **10**, **100**, or **1,000** first makes sums easier:

29 + 8
Round the **29** up to **30**: 30 + 8 = 38
Then **subtract** the 1: 38 − 1 = 37

396 + 78
Round **396** to **400**: 400 + 78 = 478
Then **subtract** the 4: 478 − 4 = 474

+

=

+

4

Gauss's Shortcut

The mathematician Carl Friedrich Gauss (1777–1855) showed his genius for sums when he was still in elementary school.
His teacher, wanting to keep the class quiet for a while, gave them a huge sum to calculate. He asked:

What is the sum of all the numbers from 1 to 100:
$1 + 2 + 3 + 4 ... + 99 + 100$

The teacher was settling in for a nap when the young Carl approached after just a few seconds with the correct answer:

5,050

How did he do it?

Gauss had noticed that the 100 numbers could be easily arranged into 50 equal pairs:

$$100 + 1 = 101$$
$$99 + 2 = 101$$
$$98 + 3 = 101$$
$$...$$
$$52 + 49 = 101$$
$$51 + 50 = 101$$

So the answer to the sum is 50 groups of 101.
$$50 \times 101 = 5,050$$
Gauss had outsmarted his teacher with math.

"Easy peasy, sir."

Taking Away

Subtraction is taking one or more numbers away from another number.

With subtraction, order matters:

$$4 - 7 = -3 \text{ but } 7 - 4 = 3$$

To see why this is, rewrite the equations as addition with negative numbers:

$$4 - 7 = 4 + (-7)$$

$$7 - 4 = 7 + (-4)$$

Each red dot cancels out a blue dot, and the **order of the calculation** changes the number of red and blue dots.

So with the first sum, **4 reds cancel out 4 blues**, leaving 3 blues left (-3). We do the same for the second sum, leaving 3 reds behind (3).

Regrouping

When subtracting, you need to **borrow from the next column** of the number if a column has a smaller number than the number to be subtracted. We make the **units larger** by **regrouping**. For instance, in 23, the "2" means **2 tens**, and the "3" means **3 ones**.

TENS (2)   ### UNITS (3)

If you **take 1** from the **tens column** and **add it** to the units, you increase the units to 13.

TENS (1)   ### UNITS (13)

6

Movie Night

Georgie and Alisha have been given **$20** to spend at the movies. The movie tickets cost **$6.75 each**, and the girls can spend the rest of the money on food and drinks.

What possible combinations can they buy?

Popcorn **$4**, Potato Chips **$2.50**, Soda **$1.25**, Candy **$1.00**

The tickets cost **$6.75 x 2 = $13.50**. **Subtracting** that from **$20** gives them **$6.50 spending money**. They need to find combinations that add up to **$6.50 or less**. They could share the popcorn and have a drink each, or they could share a drink and have popcorn and candy.

What would you choose?

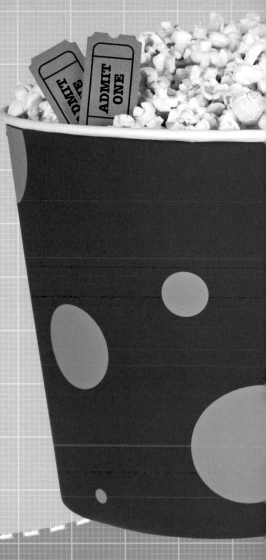

Let's put regrouping to the test by **subtracting 8 from 23**. First, you need to borrow "1" from the tens and regroup as before.

TENS (1)

UNITS (13)

Now **subtract 8** from the **units**, which gives the **answer 15**.

TENS (1)

UNITS (5)

7

Multiplying and Dividing

Learning your times tables is an important step to help you tackle more advanced math. Getting good at your tables takes practice and some hard work, but there are a few tricks that can help make the task easier.

The times table is **symmetrical**. This is because **the order** in which you **multiply numbers** does not change the result: **3 × 7 = 7 × 3**.

	1	2	3	4	5	6	7	8	9	10	11	12
1	1	2	3	4	5	6	7	8	9	10	11	12
2	2	4	6	8	10	12	14	16	18	20	22	24
3	3	6	9	12	15	18	21	24	27	30	33	36
4	4	8	12	16	20	24	28	32	36	40	44	48
5	5	10	15	20	25	30	35	40	45	50	55	60
6	6	12	18	24	30	36	42	48	54	60	66	72
7	7	14	21	28	35	42	49	56	63	70	77	84
8	8	16	24	32	40	48	56	64	72	80	88	96
9	9	18	27	36	45	54	63	72	81	90	99	108
10	10	20	30	40	50	60	70	80	90	100	110	120
11	11	22	33	44	55	66	77	88	99	110	121	132
12	12	24	36	48	60	72	84	96	108	120	132	144

Division: The Opposite of Multiplying

Division involves dividing a group into **smaller equal groups**.
Like subtraction, **order matters** with division:

4 pieces of chocolate ÷ **2** people = **2** pieces each

but
2 pieces of chocolate ÷ **4** people
= **¹/₂** piece each

Division is the opposite of multiplication, and we can use this to find answers
from multiplication tables. For instance: $3 \times 4 = 12$
From this, we also know: $12 \div 4 = 3$ and $12 \div 3 = 4$
To work out $12 \div 4$, first look along the table down the 4 column until you come
to 12. Look across the column to the left, and you will find your answer: 3.

If a number does not divide exactly by another, you can express
this as a remainder:

$$6 \div 4 = 1 \text{ remainder } 2$$

or as a fraction: $6 \div 4 = 1¹/₂$
or as a decimal: $6 \div 4 = 1.5$

How you express your result will depend on the
problem. For example, if you are dividing chocolate
bars, you can break one in half. But if you're picking
teams for a soccer game, and you have 17 players,

$$17 \div 2 = 8 \text{ remainder } 1$$

"But I prefer red!"

You cannot cut a
person in half, so
you need to give
one team a one-
player advantage
by splitting into
two unequal
groups, or leave
someone out!

Distributive Law

This law is useful when combining operations. For instance:
$$4 \times (3 + 4) = (4 \times 3) + (4 \times 4)$$
The distributive law does not apply to division:
$$12 \div (2 + 4) = 12 \div 6 = 2 \text{, but}$$
$$(12 \div 2) + (12 \div 4) = 6 + 3 = 9$$

Multiplication Tricks

A Helping Hand

Here's a trick for multiplying by 9. Hold out both hands in front of you with your fingers and thumbs straight. Numbering the fingers 1 to 10 from the left, fold the finger of the number you wish to multiply by 9. Now count the number of fingers to the left and the number of fingers to the right. That's your answer!

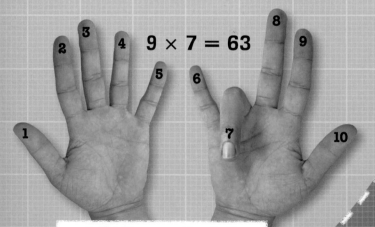

9 × 4 = 36

3 fingers on the left and 6 on the right

9 × 7 = 63

6 fingers on the left and 3 on the right

The 9 times table up to 10 shows this pattern: As the tens digit goes up one, the units digit goes down one, and both together always add up to 9.

TENS	UNITS	
0	9	0 + 9 = 9
1	8	1 + 8 = 9
2	7	2 + 7 = 9
3	6	3 + 6 = 9
4	5	4 + 5 = 9
5	4	5 + 4 = 9
6	3	6 + 3 = 9
7	2	7 + 2 = 9
8	1	8 + 1 = 9
9	0	9 + 0 = 9

Finding patterns helps with multiplication. Multiplying by 10 is easiest of all. Simply move each digit one place to the left:

$$3 \times 10 = 30$$
$$23{,}876 \times 10 = 238{,}760$$

Multiplying by 5 is the same as multiplying by 10 and halving:

$$7 \times 5 = 70 \div 2 = 35$$
$$42 \times 5 = 420 \div 2 = 210$$

Changing to 10s

When multiplying a large number by 9, first multiply the number by 10, then subtract the original number, and that's your answer:

$$83 \times 9 = 830 - 83 = 747$$
$$338 \times 9 = 3,380 - 338 = 3,042$$

When multiplying a large number by 11, first multiply by 10, then add the original number:

$$34 \times 11 = 340 + 34 = 374$$
$$63 \times 11 = 630 + 63 = 693$$

If the numbers you are multiplying are close to multiples of 10, you can round the numbers to the nearest 10, then add or subtract the remaining terms:

$$21 \times 29 = (20 + 1) \times (30 - 1)$$
$$= (20 \times 30) + (1 \times 30) + (20 \times -1) + (1 \times -1)$$
$$= 600 + 30 - 20 - 1 = 609$$

Here is a way of multiplying two two-digit numbers together. Say we want to figure out 23 × 46.

1. First, draw a group of two horizontal lines and a group of three.

2. Then draw four vertical lines and six vertical lines.

3. Bracket off the top right and bottom left, and count the points where the lines cross.

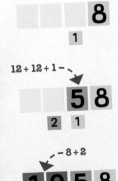

Each corner represents a different part of the calculation.

To find the answer, you start in the bottom right. This is your units. There are 18, so write down 8 in the units and carry 1.

Now add the bottom left to the top right. This is your tens. These equal 24, but you add the carried 1 to make 25. Write down 5 in the tens and carry 2.

Top left is hundreds. There are 8. Add the carried 2 and write down 10. So your answer is 1,058.

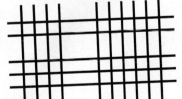

This is a way of doing long multiplication, which is also written like this:

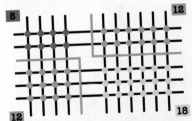

```
      23
  ×  46
```

```
       18
  +  120
  +  120
  +  800
```

1,058

Try both methods with a few different examples. Which method do you find easier?

Abacus Magic

Before the invention of electronic computers, workers were specially trained to do complicated sums with a pencil and paper. In Japan, these human computers used a soroban, which is a kind of abacus, to carry out their calculations.

Soroban Basics

Each rod on the soroban has five beads. The bead at the top represents 5, and the four beads at the bottom are 1s. Beads are added by pushing them to the middle.

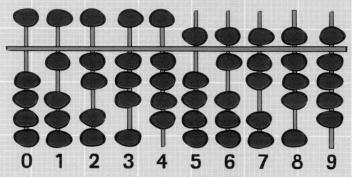

0 1 2 3 4 5 6 7 8 9

Here is the number
7,490
on a soroban:

Adding Up

Addition on a soroban is similar to addition with a pencil and paper. Here are some examples of sums.

54 + 23

First, put **5** in the **tens** column and **4** in the **units** column.

5 4

Now add **2** to the **tens** and **3** to the **units**, to give the answer: **77**

7 7

76 + 37

First put **7** in the **tens** column and **6** in the units.

7 6

Now add **3** to the **tens** column. This makes **10**, so you carry the **1** into the **hundreds** column and put the **tens** column to zero.

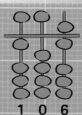

1 0 6

Add **7** to the **units**. This makes **13**, so add **1** to the **tens** column and set the **units** to **3** to give your answer: 113

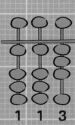

1 1 3

Champion Adders

It takes lots of practice to learn how to use a soroban quickly, but skilled users can figure out calculations at great speeds. At the 2002 World Soroban Championships, the winner added together

30 three-digit

numbers in just six seconds!

Multiplying

To do multiplication on a soroban, you need to split up the abacus. Here is the multiplication:

27 × 34

On the far right, use the first **two columns** to show **27**. Leave **a space**, then show **34** on the next **two columns**. Then leave another **space**, and show your answer in the next **three columns**:

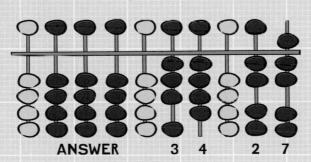

ANSWER   3 4   2 7

First multiply the **second digit** of **27** by each digit of **34**, starting with the **4**. **7 × 4 = 28**, so add this to your answer, starting with the **units** column.

0 2 8

Now, **7 × 3 = 21**, so add this to your answer, starting with the **tens** column.

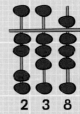

2 3 8

Next multiply the **first digit** of **27** by each digit of **34**, starting with the **4**, but remember that the **2** is in the **tens** column, so you shift one column to the left in the answers. **2 × 4 = 8**, so add this to your answer, starting with the **tens** column.

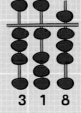

3 1 8

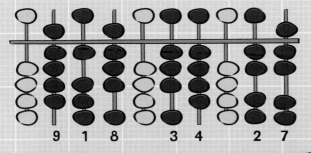

9 1 8   3 4   2 7

Finally, **2 × 3 = 6**, so add this to your answer, starting with the **hundreds** column. So the answer is **918**.

Adding Arrows

Darts players do sums very quickly in their heads. Their last throw must be a double, so they need to make sure they leave themselves a double to finish on. Through lots of practice, players learn what they need to score for each "out."

Players start by trying to score as much as they can on each throw, normally aiming for the triple bed of number 20 (T20), which scores **60**, the top score on the board with one dart. The inner bull's-eye in the center scores **50** and counts as a double of the outer bull's-eye, which scores **25**.

A game starts with **501**. Players take turns to throw three darts each, giving a top score in one turn of **180**.

When they get their score down under **231**, players need to think about leaving a **three-dart checkout** for their next throw. The highest three-dart checkout possible is **170: T20 T20 bull's-eye**. The next highest checkouts are: **167, 164, 161,** and **160**. There is no way to finish **159**; every score from **158** down can be finished in three darts.

Double Bed

Bull's-eye

Triple Bed

14

Two Darts or Three?

The highest two-dart checkout is **110**: **T20 bull's-eye.** However, the bull is the

hardest place to hit

on a dartboard, so players often prefer to use three darts instead, such as **T20 18 D16**. Miss the T20 but hit single 20, and you still have a chance to finish.

Best Doubles

It is better to leave a double of an even number. That way, if you just miss and hit the single, you're still left with a double. Double 16 is a favorite of many. Near misses leave 16, 8, 4, and 2: doubles all the way. Double 1 is called Madhouse—you'd better not miss!

"Triple twenty?"

"No, double tops!"

Nine-Dart Checkout

The minimum number of darts it takes to finish from **501** is **nine**. In total, there are **3,944 different ways** to do it, but all of them need every dart to hit its target. The most common nine-darter from 501 is this:

Throw 1: **T20 T20 T20 = 180** leaves 321
Throw 2: **T20 T20 T20 = 180** leaves 141

Throw 3:
T20 = 60
81 left
T19 = 57
24 left
D12

Possibly the hardest way to finish 501 is to throw **T20 T19 Bull** three times in a row. That gives **(60 + 57 + 50) × 3 = 167 × 3 = 501**

Can you think of other ways to finish in nine darts?

Algebra

Mathematicians often use letters to represent the values they are trying to find out. By forming equations with those letters, you can work out the values they represent.

Ancient Sums

Some of the earliest recorded algebraic equations have been found on papyrus scrolls written by an ancient Egyptian named Ahmes about 1850 BC.

One of Ahmes's main concerns was to work out a fair division of food rations. He used algebra to make sure everyone was fed.

Here is one of the problems Ahmes posed:

$$x + {}^1\!/_3 x + {}^1\!/_4 x = 2$$

Let's solve this 4,000-year-old problem for Ahmes. First, multiply both sides of the equation by 12. This gives:

$$12x + 4x + 3x = 24$$

$$19x = 24$$

Divide both sides by 19:

$$x = {}^{24}\!/_{19} = 1.26$$

to two decimal places

"Help! This doesn't add up."

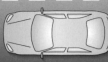

Formulas

Formulas are equations with more than one variable.

Here is a formula for converting miles per hour
(m) to kilometers per hour (k): $m = 5k/8$

A common speed limit for highways in the U.S. is 55 mph. In Spain, the limit is 120 km/h. Which is the higher limit?

To compare the two, you need to convert them to the same units. Let's use the formula to convert the miles to kilometers per hour:

$$55 = 5k/8, \text{ so } 5k = 440,$$
$$k = 88$$

The U.S. speed limit is **88 km/h**.
Spain has the higher limit.

Plotting Your Results

Graphs are a very useful way to represent equations. For equations with two variables, x and y, Cartesian coordinates plot the x value on the x-axis and the y value corresponding to that x value on the y-axis.

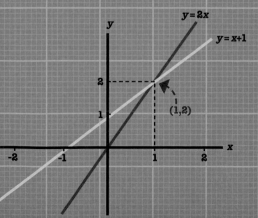

$$y = x + 1$$
$$y = 2x$$

Plotting the equations next to each other gives a solution where x and y are the same for both equations:
$x = 1$, $y = 2$

Squares, Cubes, and **Higher Powers**

Dimensions

Powers can be thought of as representing dimensions.

$2^1 = 2$
This can be thought of as two dots in one dimension joined by a line.

$2^2 = 2 \times 2 = 4$
This can be thought of as four dots in two dimensions joined by lines to form a square.

"Don't call me a square. I'm a cube!"

$2^3 = 2 \times 2 \times 2 = 8$
This can be thought of as eight dots in three dimensions joined by lines to form a cube.

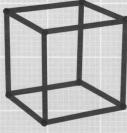

Higher Dimensions

After cubes, we run out of dimensions to show the dots, but by the power of mathematics, we can write down the numbers for higher dimensions.

$$2^4 = 2 \times 2 \times 2 \times 2 = 16$$

We cannot draw a four-dimensional shape, but one way to visualize it is with a **tesseract**.

A cube is connected to another cube in a fourth dimension. Try to imagine both cubes as being equally likely to be on the outside as on the inside of the other one. The power of mathematics is that we can deal with extra dimensions that we cannot see!

We can write powers as high as we want. 2^{100} is 2×2 **100 times**.

Multiplying Powers

$$2^3 \times 2^4 = (2 \times 2 \times 2) \times (2 \times 2 \times 2 \times 2) = 2^7 = 2^{(3 + 4)}$$

Generally, $2^a \times 2^b = 2^{(a + b)}$. Turning multiplication into addition like this makes calculations much easier.

Mathematical Shortcuts

You know the value of x^2, so what is the value of $(x + 1)^2$?

For example, $47^2 = 2{,}209$, so what is the value of 48^2?

$$48^2$$
$$= (47 \times 48) + 48$$
$$= (47 \times 47) + 47 + 48$$
$$= 47^2 + 95$$

$$48^2 = 2{,}209 + 95$$
$$= 2{,}304$$

In algebra, this can be written as:
$$(x + 1)^2$$
$$= x^2 + 2x + 1$$

It applies to any number you like. Algebra is a great way of making shortcuts.

Finding Roots

The reverse of a square is called a square root ($\sqrt{\ }$). This is the number that, multiplied by itself, would form your number.

$$2 \times 2 = 4, \sqrt{4} = 2$$

Finding square roots can be a difficult thing to do. The square root of a perfect square is a whole number:

$$\sqrt{4} = 2 \quad \sqrt{9} = 3$$
$$\sqrt{16} = 4 \quad \sqrt{25} = 5$$

However, the square roots of the whole numbers between the perfect squares cannot be written down exactly! They are **irrational numbers**, which means that they cannot be expressed in the form **a/b**, where **a** and **b** are whole numbers. We can only write down approximate numbers for them. For example, in its decimal form, $\sqrt{2}$ starts like this and goes on forever:

1.41421356237309504880
16887242096980785569

Negative Roots

Any negative number multiplied by itself is a positive number:

$$-2 \times -2 = 4$$

This means that every number actually has two square roots—one **positive** and the other **negative**:

$\sqrt{4} = 2$ or -2, written as ± 2

The graph of the equation $y = x^2$ shows two values for each value of x. It forms the shape of a parabola.

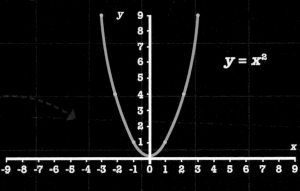

$y = x^2$

So what is the square root of a negative number? For instance, what is the value of $\sqrt{-4}$?
The square root of -1 is called i (the unit imaginary number): $i \times i = -1$
To find the square root of -4, you take the root of +4 and multiply it by i:

$$\sqrt{-4} = \sqrt{4} \times \sqrt{-1} = 2i$$

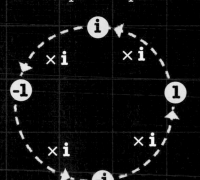

i goes in circles when you multiply it by itself:

▶ $i^2 = i \times i = -1$
▶ $i^3 = i^2 \times i = -i$
▶ $i^4 = i^3 \times i = 1$
▶ $i^5 = i^4 \times i = i$

Complex Numbers

Numbers made using i are called complex numbers. When you see color displays for music like this one, the computer is using complex numbers to work out its calculations.

The Fibonacci Sequence

In the 13th century, Leonardo Fibonacci, an Italian mathematician, posed the following problem:

At the start of the year, you have a pair of baby rabbits, one male and one female. After one month, they will be old enough to mate, and a month after that the female gives birth to another pair. Assuming that none of the rabbits die and the females mate immediately after giving birth, **how many pairs of rabbits will you have at the end of the year?**

Each new month, you have all the pairs from the last month, plus every pair that was alive the previous month has produced a new pair. Known as the Fibonacci sequence, each **new number** is **the sum of the two previous numbers** in the sequence.

The Fibonacci sequence is normally written with a zero at the start, so it looks like this:

0 1 1 2 3 5 8 13 21 34 55 89 144 233 ...

The numbers get very big very quickly. The 100th number in the sequence is:

218,922,995,834,555,169,026

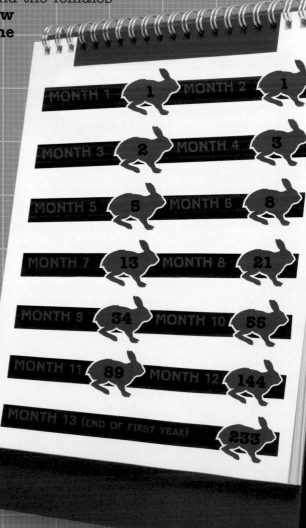

MONTH 1 — 1   MONTH 2 — 1
MONTH 3 — 2   MONTH 4 — 3
MONTH 5 — 5   MONTH 6 — 8
MONTH 7 — 13   MONTH 8 — 21
MONTH 9 — 34   MONTH 10 — 55
MONTH 11 — 89   MONTH 12 — 144
MONTH 13 (END OF FIRST YEAR) — 233

Tiling Problem

Fibonacci numbers appear in many mathematical puzzles. Here is a tiling problem you can do with a set of dominoes. Place two dominoes facedown, and arrange them into a rectangle like this.

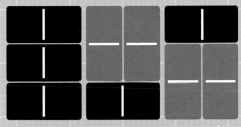

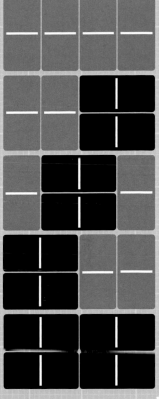

There are two ways of arranging two dominoes to fill the same rectangle.

For three dominoes, there are three ways.

For four dominoes, there are five ways.

Each time you add a domino, the number of arrangements jumps to the next number in the Fibonacci sequence.

Can you see how to arrange five dominoes in eight different ways?

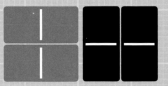

Branching Out

This plant's branches grow at a rate of 5 inches per week. When a branch is 10 inches long, it is strong enough to grow another branch. It then produces a new branch every 5 inches. As the plant grows from its first branch, each new week it produces a Fibonacci number of branches. Many real plants grow this way.

The number of petals on a flower is often a Fibonacci number. For instance, a lily has three petals, a buttercup has five, and a daisy often has 34 or 55.

23

Pascal's Triangle

Named after the French mathematician Blaise Pascal, who studied it in the 17th century, a Pascal's triangle is simple to make, but it has some astounding properties.

To make a Pascal's triangle, start with 1 at the top of a stack of hexagons like this. Each row has **one hexagon more** in it than the row above:

Continue to build each new row using the following rule: each number is **the sum** of the two numbers directly **above it**. (The 1 at the top is counted as row zero.)

1s

Counting Numbers

Triangular Numbers

Tetrahedral Numbers

Each number in one row is **used twice** to make the numbers in the next row— once for each of the two numbers below it.

```
                1
              1   1
            1   2   1
          1   3   3   1
        1   4   6   4   1
      1   5  10  10   5   1
    1   6  15  20  15   6   1
  1   7  21  35  35  21   7   1
```

The sum of each line is equal to $2^{(\text{row number})}$. So the sum of the **first row** is 2, second row 4, third row 8, fourth row 16, and so on.

Looking next at the **diagonals**, each of these also has special properties. The first diagonal (red) is just 1s. The second diagonal (yellow) is made up of the **counting numbers**. If you want to find the **square** of the counting numbers, you **add together** the number to its **right** and the number **below them** both. For example, to find the **square of 4**, you add the number **next to it**, **6**, and the number **below them**, **10**, equaling 16 = 4^2.

The third diagonal (green) contains the **triangular numbers**. These are the numbers of circles that can be arranged to **form a triangle**.

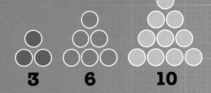

3   **6**   **10**

The fourth diagonal (blue) has the **tetrahedral numbers**. This is the number of spheres that can be arranged to form a tetrahedron.

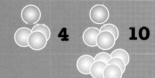

4   **10**

Combinations

Pascal's triangle provides solutions to math problems involving combinations. For example, here are all the possible ways to toss a coin four times (**H** is heads, **T** is tails):

1 HHHH

4 THHH HTHH HHTH HHHT

**6 HHTT HTHT HTTH THHT
THTH TTHH**

4 HTTT THTT TTHT TTTH

1 TTTT

This is the fourth row of Pascal's triangle. When you get to combinations with larger numbers, having a Pascal's triangle next to you makes working out the answer far easier. For instance, if you want to know the probability of getting 5 tails out of 10 tosses of a coin, you need to find the sixth entry on Row 10 (the first entry represents no tails):

1 10 45 120 210 **252** 210 120 45 10 1

There are 2^{10} total combinations, so the answer is

$$252/2^{10} = 252/1024.$$

Using a calculator gives the decimal **0.246**.

Algebra Alchemy

Here are some math tricks for you to puzzle over. Can you see how they work?

Guess Your Age

Ask a friend to think of a number between 1 and 9. **Double that number** and **add 5**. **Multiply by 50**. Now add **1,767** if your friend has already had a birthday this year, or **1,766** if the birthday is still to come.

Note: This works only if you're doing the trick in 2017. For 2018, you'll need to use 1,768 or 1,767. For each subsequent year, add 1.

Subtract the year your friend was born. You now have a **three-digit number**. The first digit is the number your friend first thought of. The second two are his or her age!

We can use algebra to see how this works. Call your initial number **n** and your birth year **b**. You can then write down the following:

$50(2n + 5) + 1766 - b$
$= 100n + (2016 - b)$
$2016 - b =$ your age.

Add that to **$100n$**, and you place **n before your age** in the hundreds column.

Counting Digits

Choose two single digits and combine them to make two different double-digit numbers. For instance: **2 and 5 combine to make 25 and 52**. Now add your single-digit numbers together and add your double-digit numbers together. Divide the larger number by the smaller number. What is the result? Try it with a few different combinations. Every time you get the same result: 11! To see why this is, line up the two-digit numbers like this, calling the digits a and b:

$$ab$$

$$ba$$

Adding these numbers together, you are adding a and b in the units column

$$(1 \times (a + b))$$

and also a and b in the tens column

$$(10 \times (a + b)).$$

This gives you **11 (a + b)**. **11(a + b) ÷ (a + b) = 11**, whatever the values of a and b.

This can be extended to three-digit numbers. You can make six different three-digit numbers from three single digits. For instance, 1, 2, and 3 can be combined to make:

213, 231, 321, 123, 312, 132

Now add your six three-digit numbers together and your three single-digit numbers together and divide one by the other. Can you explain why the answer is always 222?

Four digits can be combined to make 24 different four-digit numbers. Can you work out which answer you would get with four digits? (Hint: Each digit appears six times in each column.)

Quiz

1 What are the missing numbers from the following equations?

a) $\ldots + 77 = 100$

b) $34 + \ldots + 7 = 71$

c) $\ldots - 451 = 49$

2 If one egg carton holds 6 eggs, **how many cartons** do you need to hold 20 eggs? **How many empty spaces will there be?**

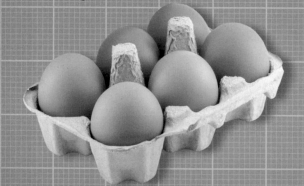

3 For the following equations, find the **value of x**.

a) $2x + \tfrac{1}{4}x = 9$

b) $x^2 = 36$

c) $\sqrt{x} = 3$

4 Which of the **following sorobans** shows the calculation

$11 \times 56?$

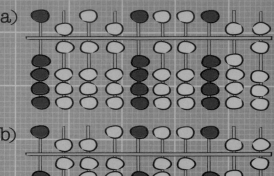

a)

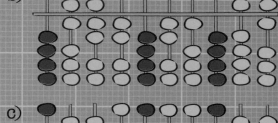

b)

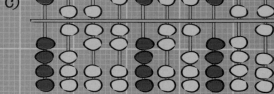

c)

5 Which of the following sorobans shows the **correct answer** to the sum

$56 + 75?$

a)   b)

c)

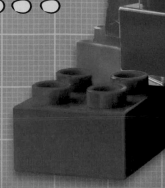

7 What is the **square root** of **-9**?

8 a) In a game of darts, you are left with

164 to finish.

How can you check out with **three darts?**

b) You have **86 left** to score with two darts.

What should you aim for

with your first dart to leave **double 16?**

c) The finish called **"Shanghai"** involves hitting

a triple, a single, and a double

of the same score. **How much is Shanghai 20 in total?**

6 You want to build a wall that is **9 bricks high** and **12 bricks long**. $^2/_3$ of the bricks will be red and $^1/_3$ of them will be blue. **How many red bricks and how many blue bricks do you need?**

9 $37^2 = 1,369$

Using the formula on page 19, what is the value of 38^2?

10 What are the **missing numbers** on this Pascal's triangle?

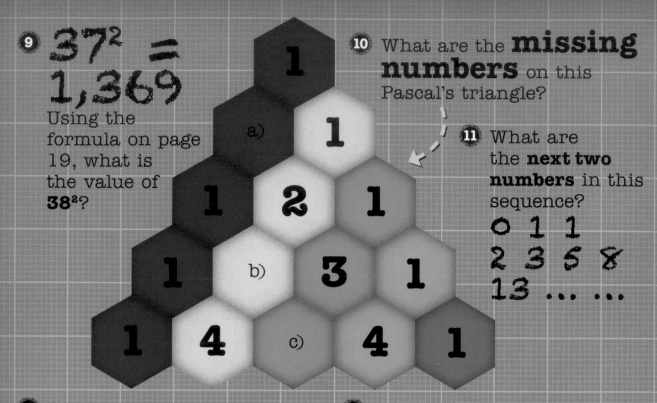

11 What are the **next two numbers** in this sequence?

0 1 1
2 3 5 8
13 ... ...

12 Arrange the numbers

1, 2, 3, 4, 5

in five boxes like these so that the sum of the numbers in the **vertical line** is the same as the sum of the numbers in the **horizontal line**.

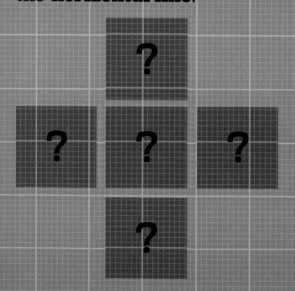

What number do they add up to?

13 Arrange the numbers

1, 2, 3, 4, 5, 6, 7, 8, 9 in squares

like these so that the total of each **row**, **column**, and **diagonal** is the same.

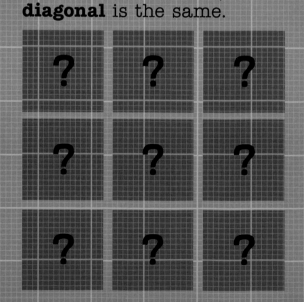

Hint: Each row, column, and diagonal should add up to 15.

Glossary

Algebra
A branch of mathematics that uses letters to represent unknown numbers, known as variables. By solving equations, the value of the letters can be calculated.

Cartesian coordinates
A way of plotting pairs of numbers on a graph. The x values run along a horizontal axis, and the y values run along a vertical axis.

Complex number
A number that contains a term that is a multiple of $\sqrt{1}$. Also known as i, $\sqrt{-1}$ is known as the unit imaginary number.

Distributive law
A law that says that multiplying one number by the sum of a group of numbers is the same as multiplying that number by each member of the group separately and adding them together: $a(b + c) = ab + ac$

Fibonacci number
A number in the Fibonacci sequence, a series of numbers each of which is the sum of the previous two numbers.

Formula
An equation that contains two or more unknown variables.

Irrational number
A number that cannot be written in the form a/b, where a and b are whole numbers. $\sqrt{2}$ is an irrational number.

Pascal's triangle
A triangle of numbers in which each number is the sum of the two numbers directly above it. It is named after the 17th-century French mathematician Blaise Pascal, but had been studied by Chinese mathematicians 400 years earlier.

Perfect square
Also known as a square number, a number that is produced by multiplying a whole number by itself.

Power
Also called an exponent, a number that tells you how many times to use another number in a multiplication. For example, in 2^4, the power is 4, meaning "multiply 2 four times."

Probability
The chance that something will happen. Probabilities can be expressed as a fraction between 0 and 1; a ratio; or a percentage. For example, the chance of getting heads when tossing a coin can be written as ½, 1:1, or 50%.

Soroban
An abacus that has five beads on each rod. One bead has the value 5, and the other four have the value 1. The soroban was developed in Japan, where it is still widely used.

Tiling
A way of arranging shapes so that they cover an area without leaving spaces.

Index

Facts for Now

Visit this Scholastic Web site for more information
on sums and to download the
Teaching Guide for this series:
www.factsfornow.scholastic.com
Enter the keywords **Super Sums**

Answers

1. a) 23 b) 30 c) 500
2. You need 4 egg cartons. There will be
4 empty spaces.
3. a) 4 b) 6 c) 9
4. a
5. b
6. 72 red, 36 blue
7. $\sqrt{9} \times \sqrt{-1} = 3i$

8. a) T20 T18 Bull, or T18 T20 Bull
b) You need to score 54, so you aim for
triple 18 c) 120
9. 1,369 + 74 + 1 = 1,444
10. a) 1 b) 3 c) 6
11. 21, 34
12. They add up
to 9. Here is one
way to do it:

13. Here's one
possible answer:

	4	
1	3	5
	2	

8	3	4
1	5	9
6	7	2